THE AWFUL JOKE BOOK

Compiled by Mary Danby
Drawings by Bryan Reading

WINGS BOOKS

New York / Avenel, New Jersey

The material in this book was compiled and adapted from
The Most Awful Joke Book Ever by Mary Danby and
The Even More Awful Joke Book by Mary Danby,
both published by Fontana Paperbacks.

This 1992 edition is published by Wings Books,
distributed by Outlet Book Company,
a Random House Company, 40 Engelhard Avenue,
Avenel, New Jersey, 07001, by arrangement with
Sterling Publishing Company, Inc.

Printed and Bound in the United States of America

Library of Congress Cataloging-in-Publication Data

Danby, Mary.
    The awful joke book / compiled by Mary Danby ; drawings by Bryan
Reading.
        p.   cm.
    ISBN 0-517-07767-1
    1. Wit and humor, Juvenile. I. Reading, Bryan. II. Title.
[PN6163.D36   1992]
828'.91402--dc20   91-37385
                                                                        CIP

8 7 6 5 4 3 2 1

CONTENTS

1. WHAT'S SO FUNNY???

I have 12 heads, five legs, six arms and 13½ toes. What am I?
  A liar.

What do you say to a South American liar?
  "I don't Bolivia (believe you)!"

STACY: I spend ages in front of the mirror admiring my beauty. Do you think it's vanity?
CASEY: No, imagination.

DAFFY: Do you like my new dress? I got it for a ridiculous price!
DILLY: You mean you got it for an absurd figure.

Did you hear about the girl with the turned up nose? Every time she sneezed, she blew her hat off.

Once there was a French count who was found guilty of spying. Even though they threatened him with torture and death, he refused to name his accomplices. Eventually, he was taken to the guillotine.

Just as the blade was about to fall, the trembling count cried, "Stop! I will tell you everything!" but it was too late. The count was beheaded. What is the moral of this story?

Don't hatchet your counts before they chicken.

WHAT'S SO FUNNY ABOUT EGGS?

What were the eggs doing in the gym?

EGGS-ERCISING

DON'T WORRY, IT'S ONLY A YOKE!

EGGS-ECUTIONER

What is a good egg to keep away from?

What did the egg get when it brought a slingshot to school?

EGGS-PELLED

WHAT'S SO FUNNY ABOUT EGGS?

What do you see when you go to a Shakespeare play put on by eggs?

EGGS-ACTING

What kind of egg buys furs and jewels?

EGGS-TRAVAGANCE

What does an egg get when it does too much work?

EGGS-HAUSTED

HOW DO YOU GET RID OF A BOOMERANG?

THROW IT DOWN A ONE-WAY STREET.

The bell sounded the end of Round Four and Battling Bob retired to his corner.

"How am I doing?" he asked his manager. "Do you think I've hurt him?"

"No," said his manager. "But keep on swinging. The breeze might give him pneumonia."

MOE: I'm even stronger than Tarzan.

FLO: Prove it.

MOE: All right. See? I can beat my chest without yelling!

WHAT MAKES A BASKETBALL COURT SO WET?

THE PLAYERS... THEY DRIBBLE A LOT.

Dopey Dan annoyed one of his teachers and was told to run one lap around the track.

An hour later, the teacher noticed that Dopey Dan was still running.

"Hey, come over here!" shouted the teacher. "I told you to run one lap."

"Sorry!" called out Dopey Dan. "I lost count."

ANGRY GAME WARDEN: You can't fish there!
LITTLE JOHNNY: I'm not fishing. I'm giving my pet worm a bath.

What happened to the silk worms who had a race?

They ended up in a tie.

Did you hear about the florist who had two children? One was a budding genius and the other was a blooming idiot.

PINKY: This match won't light.

STINKY: Why not?

PINKY: I don't know—it was all right the last time.

NIT: Today I received an anonymous letter.

WIT: Oh, who from?

How do you burn a nitwit's ear?

Phone him while he's ironing.

What happened to the nitwit who tried to blow up a bus?

He burned his lips on the exhaust pipe.

MRS. SMITH: How much are these chickens?

BUTCHER: Two dollars a pound.

MRS. SMITH: Did you raise them yourself?

BUTCHER: Yes, ma'am. This morning they were only a dollar seventy five.

A man was walking down the street with a roll of cloth under his arm, and he bumped into the local priest.

"Where did you get that roll of cloth?" asked the priest.

"I knocked it off," said the man.

"I'm sorry to hear that," said the priest, "I hope you aren't going to make a habit of it."

"Oh no, Father," said the man. "I'm going to make a sports jacket."

CUSTOMER: Would it be all right to wear this fur coat in the rain?

SALES CLERK: Madam, have you ever seen a squirrel carrying an umbrella?

What did the cheapest man in the world do when he found a box of corn plasters?

He bought himself a pair of tight shoes.

WHAT'S SMALL, ROUND, WHITE AND GIGGLES ?

A TICKLED ONION

What is the difference between a china shop and a furniture store?

One sells tea sets and the other sells settees.

CITY LADY: I'd like to buy a chicken.
FARMER: Want a pullet?
CITY LADY: Not really. I'd rather carry it.

Melvin wanted to buy a present for his mother, so he went to a pet shop and paid $200 for a mynah bird. It was a very special bird, because it could speak six languages and recite *Hiawatha* backwards.

He had the bird sent to his mother's apartment and later on he called her. "How did you like the bird?" Melvin asked.

"Fine," said his mother. "It was delicious!"

2. SEARCH ME!

What do you give a kangaroo when it's sick?
A hoperation.

What do you do to a chicken when it's sick?
You eggs-amine (examine) it.

What steps should you take if you see an escaped lion?
Very, very long ones.

What is writing on the wall of a zoo called?
Giraff-iti.

What do baby apes sleep in?
  Apri-cots.

What happened to the hyena who swallowed a bouillon cube?
  It was a laughing stock.

What lies on the ground a hundred feet up in the air?
  A dead centipede.

What do you get if you cross an alley cat with a canary?

A peeping tom.

DOTTY: How much is that canary?

PET SHOW OWNER: Ten dollars.

DOTTY: Fine, send me the bill.

PET SHOP OWNER: Sorry, madam, but you have to take the whole bird.

What says "Quick-quick?"

A duck with hiccups.

Two little girls were watching sparrows eating from a bird table.

"I wonder what they eat," said Polly, "when there's no food on the bird table."

"They eat what they can find," said Molly.

"What happens when they can't find anything?"

"Then they eat something else."

What do you call a cow eating grass?
A lawn moo-er.

What's the biggest potato in the world?
A hippo-potato-mus.

What's the difference between a hare and a rabbit?

A rabbit grows hair, but a hare doesn't grow rabbit.

TERRY: My dog's a wonderful watchdog. No stranger ever gets near our house without Fido letting us know.

JERRY: You mean he growls and barks?

TERRY: No, he crawls under the bed.

When the window cleaner arrived at the Greens' house, he was stopped in his tracks by a snarling, yapping dog.

"Don't be afraid of Poochie," said Mrs. Green. "You know the old saying, 'A barking dog never bites.'"

"Sure," said the window cleaner. "You know the old saying, I know the old saying, but does Poochie know the old saying?"

A man was walking down the street when he saw a little boy with a dog.

"Does your dog bite?" asked the man.

"No," said the boy.

The man bent down to pat the dog and the dog bit him.

"I thought you said your dog didn't bite," said the man.

"He doesn't," said the little boy, "but that's not my dog."

FLIP: I can't decide whether your dog is a setter or a pointer.

FLOP: He's a little of both. He's an upsetter and a disappointer.

I call my dog a miniature poodle. The miniature (minute you) turn your back he does a poodle.

Why does a dog wag his tail?

Because no one will wag it for him.

JEAN: Why does your dog turn around so many times before he lies down?

DEAN: He's winding himself up—he's a watchdog.

LITTLE MUFFIE: I'd like to buy a puppy. How much do they cost?

SHOPKEEPER: A hundred dollars a piece.

LITTLE MUFFIE *(shocked)*: Oh—no! How much does a whole one cost?

Why didn't the grouchy big game hunter return to his camp in the jungle?

He disagreed with something that ate him.

3. GOOD SHOW!!

WHAT IS A DUCK'S FAVORITE T.V. PROGRAM?

THE FEATHER FORECAST

What to say to a show-off:
"You ought to be on the stage. There's one leaving in five minutes."

What film star jumps over trees?
John Tree-Vaulter (Travolta).

A fat man at the movies turned to a small boy sitting behind him. "Can you see?" he asked.
"Not a thing," replied the little boy.
"Then you just keep your eyes on me," said the fat man, "and you laugh when I do."

An angry woman turned around and said to the whispering people behind her, "Do you mind? I'm trying to watch the film."
"In that case," one of them said, "you're facing the wrong way."

HE *(at movies):* Can you see all right?
SHE: Yes.
HE: You're not sitting in a draught?
SHE: No.
HE: Comfortable?
SHE: Yes, fine.
HE: Want to trade seats?

A man went to the unemployment office looking for work. He was told that he could have the part of Long John Silver in a new film version of *Treasure Island.*

"That's marvelous!" said the man. "How much will I be paid?"

"A thousand dollars a week," was the reply.

"Great!" said the man. "I start acting on Monday?"

"Oh, no," said the clerk. "On Monday you're having your leg amputated."

WHAT DO YOU CALL A HEN THAT CRACKS JOKES? A COMEDI-HEN.

ERIC: Did you like the play last night?

DEREK: I enjoyed the first act, but I didn't stay for the second.

ERIC: Why not?

DEREK: I couldn't wait that long. It said on the program, "Act Two, three weeks later."

At a talent contest, Maisie sang the Irish folk song, "Galway Bay." She noticed that a man in the front row had tears streaming down his cheeks. Afterwards she went up to him and said, "I couldn't help noticing your reaction to my song. Are you from Galway?"

"No," said the man. "I'm a musician."

FIRST MUSIC CRITIC: Did you notice how her voice filled the hall?

SECOND MUSIC CRITIC: Yes. I also noticed that a lot of people left to make room for it.

A little girl went to the opera with her father. As the conductor waved his baton, the soprano started to sing an aria.

The little girl clung to her father. "Why is that man hitting her with his stick?" she asked.

Her father laughed. "He's not hitting her, silly."

"Well, then," said the little girl, "why is she screaming?"

What is green and sings?
Elvis Parsley.

NEIGHBOR: Was that you playing the sax last night?

MUSICIAN: Yes, as a matter of fact, it was.

NEIGHBOR: Will you play solo tonight?

MUSICIAN: Solo?

NEIGHBOR: Yes, *so low* I can't hear it!

MUSIC PROFESSOR: Why do you play the same piece of music over and over again?

STUDENT: It haunts me.

MUSIC PROFESSOR: It should haunt you—you've murdered it often enough.

A glamorous blonde dressed in a bikini entered the hall of the beauty contest. One of the organizers went up to her and said, "Sorry, two-piece bathing suits are not allowed."

"Oh, dear," said the contestant. "Which piece do you want me to take off?"

How can you tell that a sculptor is unhappy?
He makes a long face.

4. SCARED STIFF

What do you call a monster that is nine feet tall, has six arms and poisonous fingernails?
  Sir.

Did you hear about the monster with pedestrian eyes? They look both ways before they cross.

What do you get if you cross a witch with an ice cube?
  A cold spell.

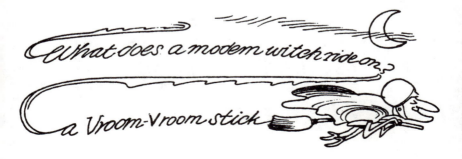

What's the difference between a deer being chased and a dwarf witch?

One is a hunted stag and the other is a stunted hag.

What would a vampire say if you offered to pull out his teeth?

"No fangs!"

If you gave Dracula a bottle of mouthwash, what would he do with it?

He'd gargoyle.

If you love Dracula, what should you do?

Join his fang club.

What do you get when you cross a watchdog and a werewolf?

A very nervous postman.

BILLY: My uncle changed his will five times in two years.

WILLY: Aha! A fresh heir fiend!

5. FOOLING WITH SCHOOLING

"Come on, Fergie," said his mother. "Hurry up and finish your breakfast or you'll be late for school."

"I don't want to go to school," said Fergie.

"But you must," said his mother.

"The teachers all hate me, and I hate them," said Fergie.

"Even so," said his mother.

"The children, too," said Fergie. "None of them like me, and I don't like them either."

"You still have to go."

"Why? Why must I?" said Fergie.

"Well," replied his mother, "for one thing, you're 55 years old, and for another, you're the principal."

TEACHER: If you were to add 89,325 and 138,561—and then multiply by 8, add 9,081 and divide by 7, what would you get?

SANDY: The wrong answer.

TEACHER: If I had ten oranges in one hand and six in the other, what would I have?
ADAM: Big hands.

TEACHER: If one and one make two, and two and two make four, what do four and four make?
VICKIE: That's not fair. You do all the easy ones and leave the hard ones for us.

TEACHER: If I had two sandwiches and you had two sandwiches, what would we have?
ROGER: Lunch.

Charlie was having trouble with subtraction.

"Now listen, Charlie," said his teacher. "You have ten fingers. If you had three fewer, what would you have?"

"No more piano lessons," he answered.

Item in the school newspaper:

Last week the school orchestra played Brahms. Brahms lost.

ART TEACHER: I asked you to draw a horse and cart. Why have you only drawn the horse?
JUDY: I thought the horse would draw the cart.

TEACHER: Can you tell me the opposite of happiness?
DENNIS: Sadness.
TEACHER: Good. Now, the opposite of sadness?
DENNIS: Gladness.
TEACHER: Very good. Now, what about the opposite of woe?
DENNIS: Giddy-up!

WHAT DO PIXIES DO AFTER SCHOOL?

GNOMEWORK.

WILMA: What did I get on my English test?
TEACHER: Well, I'll give you the good news first. You spelled your name correctly.

TEACHER *(talking about the alphabet)*: What comes after O?
GORDON: Yeah!

FATHER: What does this "O" mean on your test paper?
SON: I think it's a moon. The teacher ran out of stars.

Jack had completed his project on jet aviation and had to tell the class about it.

"Modern aircraft can do anything a bird can do and more," he finished proudly.

From the back of the room, another kid whispered, "I'd like to see one of them lay an egg."

TEACHER: What is air?
TINA: A balloon with its skin removed.

RICHIE: I've got a problem, Dad. My teacher said I have to write more clearly.

FATHER: Well, that's all right. I'm sure you can do it if you try.

RICHIE: Yes, but if I write more clearly, she'll find out I can't spell.

ZACK: I'm exhausted! I was up until midnight doing homework!

MACK: What time did you start?

ZACK: Eleven forty-five.

TEACHER: Tell me about the Iron Age.

STANLEY: Sorry, I'm a little rusty on that subject.

HISTORY TEACHER: What did Caesar say when Brutus stabbed him?

ALICE: Ouch!

Where did Martha Washington go in her 39th year?

Into her 40th.

6. GETTING WORSE

MIMI: I'll have a banana split, made with two bananas, three scoops of vanilla ice cream, chocolate sauce, chopped nuts and a big helping of whipped cream.

WAITER: Would you like a cherry on top?

MIMI: No, thanks. I'm on a diet.

DILLY: I know a girl who went on a coconut diet.

DALLY: How much weight did she lose?

DILLY: None, but you should see her climb trees.

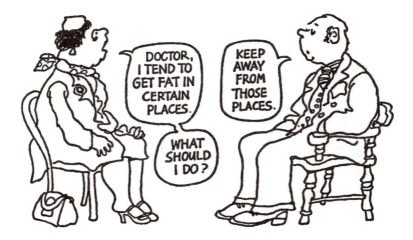

LULU: I tried one of those "I Speak Your Weight" machines today.

LESTER: What did it say?

LULU: "One person at a time, please."

I know a girl whose legs are so fat that her calves are more like cows.

Is major surgery possible on a very fat man?
Yes, but it's better on an operating table.

NIT: The surgeon removed a healthy appendix with a blunt scalpel.

WIT: What a pointless operation!

WRESTLER: I don't feel well.

DOCTOR: Get a grip on yourself.

NICK: Where are you going?

VIC: I'm on my way to the doctor's. I don't like the look of my wife.

NICK: I think I'll come with you. I don't like the look of mine either.

Did you hear about the man who went to see the eye doctor because he saw spots in front of his eyes? The eye doctor gave him glasses, and now he can see the spots much better.

When do you know for sure that someone has a glass eye?

When it comes out in conversation.

WHY WAS THE CHICKEN SICK?

BECAUSE IT HAD PEOPLE POX.

DOCTOR: You need glasses.

PATIENT: But I'm already wearing glasses.

DOCTOR: In that case, I need glasses.

PATIENT *(on telephone):* Doctor, there's something very wrong with me. My head feels squashed, my voice sounds strange, I smell something peculiar and one of my feet is cold. What could be the matter with me?

DOCTOR: You're probably wearing one of your socks on your head.

DOCTOR: Have you ever had trouble with appendicitis?

PATIENT: Only when I try and spell it.

PATIENT: I have water on the knee. What should I do?

DOCTOR: Wear pumps.

PATIENT: Doctor, can you give me something for my liver?

DOCTOR: Certainly, here's an onion.

DOCTOR: Face the window, please. Now stick out your tongue.

PATIENT: Why do I have to face the window?

DOCTOR: Because I don't like the man next door.

WHAT DO YOU GIVE A SEASICK ELEPHANT?

PLENTY OF ROOM.

PATIENT: Doctor, I feel like a goat!

DOCTOR: Hmm. . .how are the kids?

PATIENT: Doctor, I feel like a trash can!

DOCTOR: Rubbish!

MERRILL: The doctor told me to drink some lemon juice after a hot bath.

CHERYL: Did you drink the lemon juice?

MERRILL: No, I haven't finished drinking the hot bath yet.

WHAT HAPPENED TO THE HEN THAT SWALLOWED THE YO-YO?

SHE LAID THE SAME EGG THREE TIMES!

An explorer came across a witch doctor in a jungle clearing. The witch doctor was beating a drum furiously.

"What's up?" asked the explorer.

"We have no water," said the witch doctor.

"Oh, are you praying for rain?" the explorer asked.

"No," replied the witch doctor, "I'm calling a plumber."

An apple a day keeps the doctor away—if your aim is good.

GIDGET: Did you hear about the fish that had the measles?

BRIDGET: No, how is he?

GIDGET: Not bad. He only had them on a small scale.

7. BAD JOB!

Two very stupid carpenters, Lem and Clem, were making a fence. Lem was picking nails out of the box and throwing them away.

"Why are you doing that?" asked Clem.

"Well, you see," said Lem, "the heads are on the wrong ends of these nails."

"You idiot!" exclaimed Clem. "Those nails are for the other side of the fence!"

HARRY: When I grow up, I want to be a millionaire. I'll have a great big house with no bathrooms.

CARRIE: Why no bathrooms?

HARRY: I'm going to be filthy rich!

CAPTAIN: Are you happy now you're in the Navy?

ERNIE: Yes, sir!

CAPTAIN: What were you before you came into the Navy?

ERNIE: Much happier.

Before going on sentry duty, a soldier was asked by his commanding officer: "What would you do if you saw a battleship coming across the parade ground?"

The sentry was surprised to be asked a question like that, but he answered, "I'd torpedo it, sir."

"Oh, yes?" said the commanding officer. "And where would you get the torpedo?"

"From the same place you got the battleship, sir."

Why was the well-dressed man picked for the job?
He was best suited for it.

What happened to the glass blower who inhaled?
He got a pane in his chest.

What's the fastest way to learn to be a barber?
Study all the short cuts.

Did you hear about the umbrella manufacturer?
He saved his money for a sunny day.

8. HAVING A WONDERFUL TIME

FATHER: It'll be your birthday soon. How would you like to have a pocket calculator?

SON: No, thanks, Dad. I already know how many pockets I have.

BONNIE: Are you getting a new hairdo for the party?

CONNIE: No, I'm having a henna-do.

BONNIE: What's a henna-do?

CONNIE: It runs around and says, "Cluck, cluck!"

Did you hear about the Scot who washed his kilt and couldn't do a fling with it?

Why were the two butterflies turned away from the dance?
It was a mothball.

How do hens and roosters dance?
Chick to chick.

DANCER: Can you stretch the music out a little longer?

CONDUCTOR: Sorry, my friend. This is a dance band, not a rubber band.

WHAT IS A
FROG'S FAVORITE
DRINK ?

CROAKA-COLA.

What do you call a man wearing ear-muffs?
Anything you like. He can't hear you.

SALLY *(who has taken her little brother to a birthday party)*: That's the fourth time you've gone back for ice cream and cake. Aren't you embarrassed?

LITTLE BROTHER: Why should I be? I told everyone it's for you.

MILLY: How did you make this cake?

TILLY: Here's the recipe. I cut it out of a magazine.

MILLY: Are you sure you read the right page? The other side tells how to make a rock garden.

What's a cannibal's favorite game?
Swallow the Leader.

What's a parrot's favorite game?
Mono-polly.

MOTHER: How was the party?

WILLIAM: I didn't go. The invitation said, "From three to six," and I'm seven.

MOTHER: Did you thank Mrs. Jones for the lovely party?

HEDY: No. The boy leaving before me thanked her, and Mrs. Jones said, "Don't mention it," so I didn't.

LONG-STAYING GUEST: I can imitate any bird.

HOST (*tired*): How about a homing pigeon?

What's the difference between a gossip and a mirror?

One speaks without reflecting and one reflects without speaking.

What kind of nut sneezes the most?

Cashew!

The old lady was delighted with the gift the boy brought her.

"I'll stop by and see your mother tomorrow," she said, "and thank her for this lovely pie."

"Um, if you don't mind," the boy said nervously, "could you thank her for two pies?"

9. HERE COMES TROUBLE!

GUY: My dad's in prison because he made big money.

CY: How much?

GUY: About a quarter of an inch too big.

MINISTER: If you found a twenty dollar bill lying on the pavement, would you keep it?

WESLEY: Oh, no, sir.

MINISTER: I'm glad to hear you say that. What *would* you do with it?

WESLEY: I'd spend it.

I know someone whose folks are in the iron and steel business. His mother irons and his father steals.

Why did they give the postman the sack?
To put letters in.

FRED: Where did you get that beautiful stuffed lion?

NED: In Africa. I went on a hunting expedition with my cousin Bert.

FRED: What's he stuffed with?

NED: Cousin Bert.

What's the difference between a church bell and a thief?

One peals from the steeple and the other steals from the people.

Did you hear about the thief who was caught in a rubber factory?

The judge sent him up for a stretch.

FOREMAN OF THE JURY: We find the defendant not guilty.

DEFENDANT: Hey, judge, does that mean I get to keep the money?

FIRST BURGLAR: The cops are coming! Quick! Jump out the window!

SECOND BURGLAR: But we're on the 13th floor!

FIRST BURGLAR: This is no time to be super-stitious!

Sam was hoping to join the police force. At his interview, he was asked:

"If you were alone in a police car, being chased by a gang of desperate criminals in another car doing 50 miles an hour along a winding country road, what would you do?"

Sam looked puzzled for a moment and then answered, "Sixty."

Why did the gangster cut the legs off his bed?
So he could lie low.

BARBER: Was your tie red before you came in here?

CUSTOMER: No.

BARBER: Uh-oh.

10. THE GREAT OUTDOORS

A man at the seashore stormed over to a woman who was sitting by the water.

"Madam," he said angrily, "is that your little boy who's burying my clothes in the sand?"

"Certainly not," she replied. "My son is standing in the water—sailing your hat in the surf!"

The little boy was walking up and down the beach crying and saying, "I'm lost, I'm lost, I can't find my mommy."

Several people tried to console him. They gave him candy and bought him ice cream.

After a while, somebody came along and said, "It's all right, little boy. I know where your mommy is."

"So do I," whispered the little boy. "Please lower your voice and go away."

WHY DOES A MOTHER KANGAROO HATE RAIN?

BECAUSE THE CHILDREN HAVE TO PLAY INSIDE.

We went on vacation for a week and it only rained twice: once for three days and once for four.

Two mice were out walking. One fell in the river.
What did the other one do?

He applied mouse-to-mouse resuscitation.

The little boy, playing in the park, had lost his mother. After a while, he approached a policeman and asked, "Excuse me, but did you happen to see a lady without a kid like me?"

CAROL: Did you have a good vacation?
DARRYL: No. It rained every day.
CARROL: Then how did you get that great tan?
DARRYL: That's no tan—that's rust.

JANE: Is it safe to swim here? I'm afraid of crocodiles.

DANE: Oh, you don't have to worry about them. The sharks scare them away.

Dopey Dick was looking for a good place to water ski. But he gave up. He couldn't find a sloping lake.

11. HE AND SHE

"Dearest Mabel," wrote Herman, "I would swim the mighty ocean for one look in your deep blue eyes. I would walk through a wall of flame for one touch of your tiny hand. I would leap the deepest chasm for a word from your ruby lips. As always, your Herman. P.S. I'll be over Sunday night if it doesn't rain."

Because his was an undying love.

When a lady faints, what number will restore her?

You must bring her two.

SLEAZY SID: Hi, Cutie! Say, you're really something special! What big blue eyes! I could live in those eyes!

SLOPPY SUE: Well, you'd feel right at home. There's a sty in one of them.

HE: I dreamed I danced with the world's most beautiful woman.

SHE: What was I wearing?

HE: I'm looking for a beautiful girl.

SHE: Well, here I am!

HE: Good, you can help me look.

Jonathan had overstayed his welcome at his girlfriend's house.

"You'd better leave now," she said. "My father has a habit of taking things apart to see why they won't go."

DULCIE: Would you like to hear about a piano, a stormy sea and you?
DUNCAN: All right.
DULCIE: A piano makes music, a stormy sea makes you sick, and you make me sick.

NICOLA: I've proposed to four different men without avail.
NICHOLAS: Next time, try wearing a veil.

What did the plank of wood say to the electric drill?
"You bore me."

FIRST MONSTER: What lovely eyes you have!
SECOND MONSTER: Thanks, they were a
  Christmas present.

Why didn't the suitor win the princess's hand?
He didn't suit her.

PSYCHIATRIST: I wouldn't worry too much about
  your son making mud pies.
MOTHER: Well, I do worry, and so does his wife.

TIM: What kinds of wood make a match?
KIM: That's easy. He would and she would.

What happened when the dentist married the manicurist?
They fought tooth and nail.

WHAT DO YOU CALL TWO
SPIDERS WHO JUST GOT
MARRIED ?
newlywebs

What did the electrician's wife say when her husband came home after midnight?
"Wire you insulate?"

HE: I think the laundry must have sent me the wrong shirt. The collar is so tight I can hardly breathe.
SHE: Don't be so silly. You've got your head through the buttonhole.

ELVIN: I need a new jacket.
ESTHER: But your sheepskin jacket can't be that bad. You've only worn it for six months.
ELVIN: Yes, but look how long the sheep wore it.

A snake-charmer married an undertaker. As a wedding present they received a pair of towels marked "Hiss" and "Hearse."

12. GOING OUT TO EAT

CUSTOMER: Waiter, what's this fly doing in my ice cream?

WAITER: Looks like it's learning to ski.

CUSTOMER: Waiter, there's a fly swimming in my soup!

WAITER: Then I must have given you too much soup. It should only be wading.

CUSTOMER: Waiter, there's a fly in my stew.

WAITER: They don't care what they eat, do they?

CUSTOMER: Waiter, why does my tea have a fly in it?

WAITER: For a cup of tea that costs 60 cents, what do you want to have fall into it—an elephant?

PENNY: I just swallowed a fly.
BENNY: Hadn't you better take something for it?
PENNY: No, let it starve.

CUSTOMER: Waiter, there's a bee in my soup!
WAITER: Yes, sir, it's the fly's day off.

CUSTOMER: Why is this piece of pie all smashed up?
WAITER: Well, sir, you said, "Apple pie and step on it," so I did.

CUSTOMER: Waiter, this soup is disgusting.
WAITER: How do you know?
CUSTOMER: A little swallow told me.

CUSTOMER: I can't eat this steak. Call the manager.
WAITER: It's no use, sir. He can't eat it either.

Why does the Statue of Liberty stand in New York harbor?

Because it can't sit.

WAITER: I have boiled tongue, fried liver and pigs' feet.

CUSTOMER: I'm not interested in your medical problems, just bring me a sandwich and a cup of coffee.

CUSTOMER: Why are you cleaning up that spilled soup with a piece of cake?

WAITER: It's a sponge cake, sir.

HOTEL MANAGER: Some of our guests seem to regard our cutlery as a form of medicine.

DINER: What do you mean?

HOTEL MANAGER: To be taken after meals.

CUSTOMER: The service in this restaurant is so slow—

WAITER: How slow is it?

CUSTOMER: The service in this restaurant is so slow that I ordered a poached egg on toast—and by the time it got to the table it was a chicken sandwich.

Did you hear about the man who was carving some cold meat when it fell on the floor? It was a slip of the tongue.

CUSTOMER: Are you supposed to tip the waiters around here?

WAITER: Well, yes, sir.

CUSTOMER: Then how about tipping me? I've been waiting for two hours.

Sign outside of restaurant:

> DON'T STAND OUTSIDE AND BE
> MISERABLE. COME INSIDE AND GET
> FED UP.

The new waitress in the restaurant dropped a load of plates. Then, a little later, she dropped another load.

The manager called out, "More plates?"

"No," she answered, "Less."

A man walked into a pizza parlor and ordered an anchovy pizza. Then he walked up the wall, across the ceiling, down the wall and out the door.

"How strange," said one of the customers.

"Yes," remarked the man at the counter. "He usually orders pepperoni."

WAITER: Haven't I seen you somewhere before?

FILM STAR *(pleased)*: You may have seen me in the movies.

WAITER: That may be it. Where do you usually sit?

FIRST CANNIBAL: We had burglars last night.

SECOND CANNIBAL: Oh really?

FIRST CANNIBAL: Yes, and you know, they don't taste half as good as missionaries.

Why did the sword swallower eat pins and needles?

Because he was on a diet.

"A hot dog is the noblest dog of all."

   "Why is that?"

"Because it feeds the hand that bites it."

MANNY: Did you hear about the potato farmer who crossed a sponge with a potato?

FANNY: No—what were the potatoes like?

MANNY: They tasted disgusting, but they were great for soaking up gravy.

WHAT WAS THE WORM DOING IN THE CORNFIELD? GOING IN ONE EAR AND OUT THE OTHER.

The village idiot was sitting on a wall when Farmer Gibbs came by with a truckload of manure.

"Hey," called the village idiot, "what are you going to do with that load of manure?"

"Put it on my strawberries," Farmer Gibbs called back.

"And they call *me* crazy," the village idiot chuckled, "I always use cream."

13. ON THE WAY

Dopey Dan went for a ride on a train. After a while, he went to get a snack and began talking with another passenger.

"I always feel sick when I sit with my back to the engine," he said. "And I'm sitting that way today."

"Why don't you ask the person opposite you to change places?" the passenger suggested.

"Well, I would," said Dopey Dan, "but no one's sitting there."

What do you get if you cross the Atlantic Ocean with the Titanic?

Only part way.

NAVY RECRUITING OFFICER: Would you like to go into submarines?

RECRUIT: No, sir! I don't want to have anything to do with ships that sink on purpose!

GLADYS: My husband drives like lightning.
EDNA: You mean he goes very fast?
GLADYS: No, he's always striking trees.

The woman in the two-tone convertible stalled at the traffic light, and spent some time trying to re-start the engine. Meanwhile, the lights went through their sequence of red, green, yellow; red, green, yellow, and so on.

A policeman walked up to the car and said, "What's the matter, madam? Don't we have any colors you like?"

As the man said when he dented his new car:
   "Well, that's the way the Mercedes-Benz."